THE LITTLE
BOOK OF
FARTS

THE LITTLE BOOK OF FARTS

This edition copyright © Summersdale Publishers Ltd, 2018
First published as *Fartopedia* in 2015

With text by Anna Martin and Stephen Brownlee

An Hachette UK Company
www.hachette.co.uk

Summersdale Publishers Ltd
Part of Octopus Publishing Group Limited
Carmelite House
50 Victoria Embankment
LONDON
EC4Y 0DZ

www.summersdale.com

Printed and bound in China

ISBN: 978-1-78685-566-4

THE LITTLE BOOK OF FARTS

CONTENTS

INTRODUCTION

We all do it, although some of us fart quietly in private while others trump proudly for all to enjoy — in a board meeting, on the train or in a lift (my personal favourite). For the first time, after years of painstaking research, farts have been distilled and explained in the world's first dictionary for dedicated farters. Keep it with you at all times so on the next occasion you hear or smell a trump you'll be able to identify it — you'll wonder how you ever lived without this fabulous tome.

FART RATINGS

Smelliness Rating: Farts that score highly in this rating are bound to make your eyes water. Some farts are so vile you'd think they'd be accompanied by a green fog instead of just the putrid stench that fills the room. A traditional way of escaping this element of a fart is a good old-fashioned clothes peg on the nose, so the smell of a fart in this book is measured in pegs.

Loudness Rating: Farts that excel
here will certainly not go quietly,
announcing their arrival like their
own personal herald. Loud and proud,
this rating is measured in trumpets.

Messiness Rating: Farts that are strong
in this category do not discriminate
between solids, gases and liquids — they
can come in a variety of smells, shapes
and forms. The messier a fart is, the

more likely you'll need a change of pants, so this aspect is measured in pants.

Overall: This rating is based on a combination of each of the above criteria as well as a certain *je ne sais quoi*, which could be described as the general effect of the fart. As a fart is nothing without its maker, the overall rating is measured in bums.

THE REAL STINKERS

These farts are the pinnacle of putrid. They're bound to get your eyes watering, your nostrils flaring and your gag reflex, er, flexing...

THE LINGERER (AKA THE HOUSE GUEST)

SMELLINESS RATING:

LOUDNESS RATING:

MESSINESS RATING:

OVERALL:

At first, this fart seems like
your everyday flatulence. But when,
20 minutes later, it's still there, you know
you have a problem. If you release one
of these in your own home then your
only option is moving out. Either it
goes or you do, and it's not shifting!

THE STINKY HOUDINI

SMELLINESS RATING:

LOUDNESS RATING:

MESSINESS RATING:

OVERALL:

A surreptitious release of silent-but-deadly gas into a crowded area. The secret to the success of this fart is to time the release so that a quick escape can be made before the odour develops maximum stinkiness. Failure to flee the vicinity could lead to a fate worse than death: falling victim to your own noxious cloud.

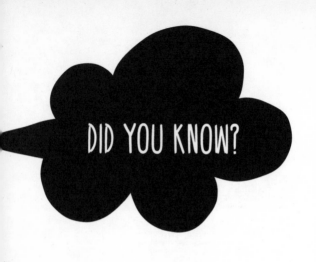

DID YOU KNOW?

It is only one per cent of the gas
that makes up farts that gives
them their smell. It's the sulphur
content in hydrogen sulphide that
gives them their unique aroma.

 # EGG BARON

SMELLINESS RATING:

LOUDNESS RATING:

MESSINESS RATING:

OVERALL:

This one is particularly nausea-inducing. The lingering smell of rotten eggs will not only permeate your clothes but those of unfortunate bystanders. The only way to cover this one up is to call cheerily, 'Egg sandwiches, anyone?' as you whip out a lunch platter from your back pocket. Yum!

AIR BISCUIT

SMELLINESS RATING:

LOUDNESS RATING:

MESSINESS RATING:

OVERALL:

This fart is so potent that you can almost hold it, like a biscuit. You might not want to dip this particular treat in your tea, though.

 # GASSY ASSASSIN

SMELLINESS RATING:

LOUDNESS RATING:

MESSINESS RATING:

OVERALL:

This silent but deadly flump is a
classic. Letting one of these go is a
pleasure, and the smellier the better
as no one will know it's you, unless
you're caught high-fiving yourself.

CULTURED FARTS

Like all things, farts are not created in a vacuum (though we sometimes wish they were!). They are influenced by the culture we enjoy, be it music, art, film or any other form of expression. These emissions truly put the 'f' in 'art'.

GONE WITH THE WIND

SMELLINESS RATING:

LOUDNESS RATING:

MESSINESS RATING:

OVERALL:

If there was an Oscar dedicated to outstanding achievement in performing farts, this one would sweep the board. It's evergreen; a fart that stands the test of time and demonstrates the best and worst of the human condition — often the result of mixing your drinks and stopping off for a combination kebab with all the extras on your way home (something we must all experience at least once in a lifetime). In the words of Margaret Mitchell, 'It was better to know the worst than to wonder.'

FARTING ETIQUETTE

When mingling at a social event, if a silent fart slips out, leave the vicinity abruptly as it happens. It will take a few seconds for the odour to leave your trousers. Once it's gone, you can get back to mingling and leave the fart behind.

 # THE WIND IN THE WILLOWS

SMELLINESS RATING: 🪵🪵🪵

LOUDNESS RATING: 🎺🎺

MESSINESS RATING:

OVERALL: ⧽⧽| ⧽⧽|

The sounds of an English summer... ducks
quacking, frogs croaking, leather on
willow, but, 'What's that noise?
It sounds like a tiny trumpet,' says
your companion, to which you reply,
'No, that's the wind in the willows...'

NIGHT OF THE
LIVING FARTS

SMELLINESS RATING:

LOUDNESS RATING:

MESSINESS RATING:

OVERALL:

This fart is the perfect accompaniment to a night on the sofa, a dirty takeaway and a box set of comedy-horror films, because you never know when the next anal belch is going to strike.

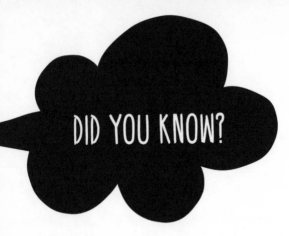

DID YOU KNOW?

An average fart is made up of:

58% nitrogen

21% hydrogen

9% carbon dioxide

7% methane

4% oxygen

1% hydrogen sulphide

 # 50 SHADES OF BROWN

SMELLINESS RATING: 🪵🪵🪵

LOUDNESS RATING: 🎺🎺🎺

MESSINESS RATING: 👙👙

OVERALL: 💨 💨 💨

A bodice-ripping fart only to be released in the presence of consenting adults, with clear boundaries and safe words in place. If your tastes are very singular, this fart will surely get your inner goddess farting.

FEEL THE FORCE!

SMELLINESS RATING:

LOUDNESS RATING:

MESSINESS RATING:

OVERALL:

A fart that is so loud it can be felt a long time ago, in a galaxy far, far away. The perfect way to tell someone, 'No, I am your farter!'

 # BUM RAP

SMELLINESS RATING:

LOUDNESS RATING:

MESSINESS RATING:

OVERALL:

Do a one-eighty with your cap and drop your waistband to your knees, because this trouser whistle is all in the presentation. Swagger to a hip-hop beat 'til it drops out and round it off with a freestyle rap.

SPINAL PARP

SMELLINESS RATING:

LOUDNESS RATING:

MESSINESS RATING:

OVERALL:

See, most farts go up to ten, but this fart, this fart goes up to eleven. That's one fartier... After getting a whiff of this, you'll wish you just smelled the glove.

FARTING ETIQUETTE

If you release a stinky emission whilst
out walking the dog then it's always
fine to blame the pooch. With their
cute little tails and playful demeanour,
they can get away with anything.

MUSICAL FARTS

Creative farts come in many forms, but these farts all have an undoubtable musicality, endearing them to the hearer and lightening the soul, like a choir of angels singing on top of a particularly whiffy rubbish tip.

TOILET TUNES

SMELLINESS RATING:

LOUDNESS RATING:

MESSINESS RATING:

OVERALL:

Everyone enjoys busting a few Toilet Tunes. If you discover you have an audience waiting outside to use the convenience, act like you've performed the gig of your life and take a bow as you make your exit. You could even offer a ticket to your next gig, or sign a piece of toilet paper for them — wash your hands first, though.

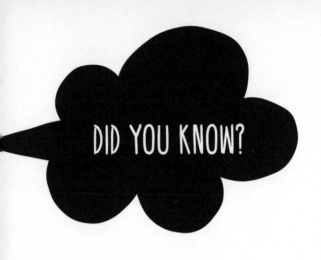

DID YOU KNOW?

An ancient Japanese piece of
artwork (or 'fartwork') from
the Edo period entitled *He-Gassen*
(*The Fart War*) depicts men and women
attacking each other with farts.

TRUMPET CHORUS

SMELLINESS RATING: 🪵🪵🪵🪵

LOUDNESS RATING: 🎺🎺🎺🎺

MESSINESS RATING: 👙👙

OVERALL: 𝄞| 𝄞| 𝄞| 𝄞|

The ability to produce a melody from your bottom is the Holy Grail for connoisseurs of anal wind. Whilst many farts sound like an off-key trumpet, a Trumpet Chorus is harmonious, like a chorus of angels — but they still stink!

SING THE ANAL ANTHEM

SMELLINESS RATING:

LOUDNESS RATING:

MESSINESS RATING:

OVERALL:

A post-pub favourite — when
you're too drunk to sing Oasis's
greatest hits, your bum can do it for you.
A 'Champ-anal Supernova', if you will.

 FROG CHORUS

SMELLINESS RATING: 🪵🪵

LOUDNESS RATING: 🎺🎺🎺

MESSINESS RATING: 👙👙

OVERALL: ⸮⸮ ⸮⸮ ⸮

This is the baritone of farts — a sound so deep that you can feel the floor vibrate. Like opera singing, it takes years to hone this skill and produce such silky tones — many have tried and most have ended up destroying their underwear.

THE ASCENDER

SMELLINESS RATING:

LOUDNESS RATING:

MESSINESS RATING:

OVERALL:

Named for its tone, The Ascender
starts off as a deep, guttural rumble,
but rises in pitch to end as a squeak —
like air being released from a balloon.
It can be achieved through precision
movement of the butt cheek, expert
choice in seating material, or simply
the fart gods smiling on you that day.
For optimum impact, the fart should
last for at least three seconds.

BROWN BRASS CHOIR

SMELLINESS RATING:

LOUDNESS RATING:

MESSINESS RATING:

OVERALL:

The rousing sound of a brass band emanating from your nether regions will make you misty-eyed... even if you weren't brought up in a small coal-mining town.

 # PARPSICHORD

SMELLINESS RATING:

LOUDNESS RATING:

MESSINESS RATING:

OVERALL:

As melodious as it is malodorous —
a sound to delight the aural and the anal,
erm, bits. This one will really impress the
future mother-in-law when you're asked
to perform a post-Sunday-lunch recital.

DID YOU KNOW?

In 2011, the Malawi government introduced new legislation intended to prohibit fouling of the air. Journalists interpreted this as a ban on breaking wind and the news went global, with Malawi's minister of justice initially backing up the claims, then later retracting his comments.

FART ATTACKS

With great fart power comes great responsibility, which these farts blatantly flout, utilising nefarious butt gas to inflict harm on others. Tut tut.

MAGIC CUPCAKE

SMELLINESS RATING:

LOUDNESS RATING:

MESSINESS RATING:

OVERALL:

As gifts go, this one stinks!
Cup your hand beneath your rear
end to 'catch' your fart, then quickly
fling it at the desired recipient. They
won't forget this gift in a hurry!

 # DUTCH OVEN

SMELLINESS RATING:

LOUDNESS RATING:

MESSINESS RATING:

OVERALL:

The old farting-in-bed-and-insisting-
your-lover-bathes-in-your-scent-by-
inviting-them-under-the-covers trick.
A classic fart, though not recommended
if you're trying to impress a new love,
unless they like that sort of thing.

THE DIRTY PROTEST

SMELLINESS RATING:

LOUDNESS RATING:

MESSINESS RATING:

OVERALL:

A fart comprised primarily of spite (and methane). Typically released during periods of intense annoyance and irritation, such as during a pretentiously avant-garde modern dance performance or a slideshow of your co-worker's 500 holiday snaps.

THE 'I DROPPED
MY PENCIL'

SMELLINESS RATING:

LOUDNESS RATING:

MESSINESS RATING:

OVERALL:

A dastardly weaponisation of your digestive gases. Simply walk past your seated victim, 'accidentally' drop your pencil/didgeridoo/pot plant (whichever best suits the situation), bend over to pick it up and BAM, direct hit! Be warned before using this fart: the attack is so blatant that retaliation will almost certainly be forthcoming, so a clean getaway is necessary.

TRAVEL FARTS

By air, by rail, by road and by bike, you can try to escape these farts, but they'll always be with you on your journey.

 # COMMUTE SUICIDE

SMELLINESS RATING:

LOUDNESS RATING:

MESSINESS RATING:

OVERALL:

The act of passing wind on a busy commuter train. When you're so squashed in that your feet no longer touch the floor, it's a pretty safe bet that no one will know it was you. Just make sure you keep a straight face.

PRESSURE
RELEASE VALVE

SMELLINESS RATING:

LOUDNESS RATING:

MESSINESS RATING:

OVERALL:

A fart you're most likely to encounter after a 12-hour coach journey without a working toilet on board and with no rest stops. There's only so long you can hold your bowels before something's got to give. Summoning otherworldly powers, your body infuses the essence of your withheld monster poo into a fart, and inflicts it upon your fellow travellers. That'll teach them to fall asleep on your shoulder and kick the back of your chair.

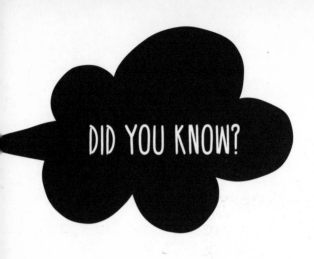

DID YOU KNOW?

The reason that people are
less bothered by their own farts
than other people's is simply that
they become accustomed to them.
Every digestive system is different
and therefore everyone's farts
have a slightly different odour.

 # TURDULANCE

SMELLINESS RATING: 🌭🌭🌭

LOUDNESS RATING: 📯📯📯📯

MESSINESS RATING: 👙👙

OVERALL: ⸮⸮| ⸮⸮| ⸮⸮|

This is what happens when you hold in your flatus for too long on a long-haul flight because you don't want to use those horrible plane toilets. Adopt the brace position and ensure your seatbelt is fastened.

PARPCYCLE

SMELLINESS RATING:

LOUDNESS RATING:

MESSINESS RATING:

OVERALL:

There's nothing like a brisk bike ride to reinvigorate the senses, get your blood flowing and get some fresh air in your lungs. But what to do if you find yourself halfway up a monster of a hill, quickly running out of steam? Let one rip and parp your way to the top of the hill. So much for that fresh air...

DIGESTIVE JUSTICE

There's a phrase in computing which goes 'garbage in, garbage out'. This phrase can be applied with as much accuracy to farting. As you will reap what you sow, so you will fart what you eat.

AIR ON A
G-STRING

SMELLINESS RATING:

LOUDNESS RATING:

MESSINESS RATING:

OVERALL:

A wedding favourite, but for all the wrong reasons. Who would have thought consuming 30 egg vol-au-vents and a full case of lager could have such an effect?

THE FESTIVE FART

SMELLINESS RATING:

LOUDNESS RATING:

MESSINESS RATING:

OVERALL:

We all like to indulge in a sprout or ten at Yuletide, but the resultant carolling that warbles out of your rear is sadly not so desirable. Only let this one go when you're surrounded by people who really love you, and if you happen to be in the UK, try to hold it in during The Queen's Speech unless you can fart the national anthem.

DID YOU KNOW?

The farts of female southern
pine beetles contain a pheromone
called frontalin, which they use
to call other members of their
species. The pheromone is especially
attractive to males of the species.

 # SILENT STINK

SMELLINESS RATING:

LOUDNESS RATING:

MESSINESS RATING:

OVERALL:

It's doubtful that even you will foresee
the arrival of this particular popper,
as it slips out like the devil in velvet
trousers. 'Oh, I wish I hadn't eaten
that fridge pack of beans all to myself!'
you might say, and you'd be right.

FARTNADO

SMELLINESS RATING:

LOUDNESS RATING:

MESSINESS RATING:

OVERALL:

Everyone has a particular food that they shouldn't go within ten feet of (mine's onions, in case you were wondering), and should a mere morsel of said food pass your lips — sometimes through no fault of your own — all hell breaks loose. It's as though the great storm from *The Wizard of Oz* is swirling in your lower bowel, only there won't be a yellow brick road at the end of it — more like a brown one.

THE COLON-SHAKER

SMELLINESS RATING: 🪵🪵🪵

LOUDNESS RATING: 🎺🎺

MESSINESS RATING: 👙👙👙

OVERALL: 💨 💨 💨

The body's reaction to a severe change
in diet, usually experienced on holiday.
If prone to this reaction, you're in a
no-win situation; you're either gurning and
farting for your whole holiday or you're
the unadventurous tourist who keeps
asking restaurants if they serve chips.

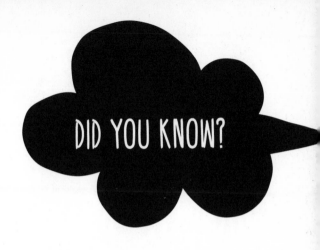

DID YOU KNOW?

The word 'fart' has been around for a very long time, and was present in many different Indo-European languages. Another word for farting that has been lost through time is 'fist', which, through a derogatory term for lapdogs, we get the word 'feisty'.

DANGER FARTS

Farts for the risk-takers of the world,
the true mavericks who are willing to
take their own lives (and the lives of
those around them) into their hands
(or, more accurately, butt cheeks) and
gamble it all on that one majestic parp.

 # RING STINGER

SMELLINESS RATING:

LOUDNESS RATING:

MESSINESS RATING:

OVERALL:

Hot winds down below can lead
to this complaint, and the Ring
Stinger particularly smarts. Prepare
for this one after a hot curry or
spicy Mexican by putting a few rolls
of toilet paper in the fridge.

PEAKY BLINDER

SMELLINESS RATING:

LOUDNESS RATING:

MESSINESS RATING:

OVERALL:

This fart should carry a health warning and must not be attempted within a confined space — unless you wish to ape the defence mechanism of a skunk against your foe, as the smell will render them temporary blind as they pull down their flat cap to cover their nostrils.

 # FLAMETHROWER

SMELLINESS RATING: 🍫

LOUDNESS RATING: 🎺 🎺

MESSINESS RATING: 👙 👙

OVERALL: 💨 💨 💨 💨

Lighting a fart is a rite of passage —
the anal passage! To avoid a terrible
escalation, this fart should not be
attempted near any flammable upholstery
or in forests during dry seasons.

FARTING ETIQUETTE

In the event of a silent fart in a situation you can't escape from, wait for 20 seconds after smelling your own fart. After this time, look around disgustedly as if to say, 'who farted?' The delay will mean that those sitting near you will think that the offending smell reached them before you, thereby clearing your name as the culprit.

N.B. if your chair has a solid bottom, rather than holes or mesh, ensure you add a few seconds on to the delay as the fart will not exit so easily.

BLOW THE HOUSE DOWN

SMELLINESS RATING:

LOUDNESS RATING:

MESSINESS RATING:

OVERALL:

Not to be performed on a fault line —
imagine the carnage — and it's most
unlikely that you'll be able to claim it on
insurance, unless you can convince your
broker that a fart is an Act of God.

RECREATIONAL FARTING

You know the saying: all rest and no play makes Jack a dull farter (that's definitely how it goes). These farts are for the jesters and playful tricksters, farting with reckless abandon and glee.

PULL MY FINGER

SMELLINESS RATING:

LOUDNESS RATING:

MESSINESS RATING:

OVERALL:

Oh, go on, you know you want to.
That old party trick of farting on
command is a life skill — perhaps
worthy of going on the CV.

PULL MY LEG

SMELLINESS RATING:

LOUDNESS RATING:

MESSINESS RATING:

OVERALL:

This is university-level farting. It's one that will make a lasting impression at any social event, especially if you drop this devil during that all-important impression-making first week. Prepare for it with the standard student fare of corned beef and beans, loosen up with some lunges and wear baggy clothing. You legend!

 # YOGA FART

SMELLINESS RATING: 🗞️🗞️

LOUDNESS RATING: 🎺🎺

MESSINESS RATING: 👙

OVERALL: 〵〵| 〵〵|

It's an occupational hazard when you're doing the downward dog, the tree pose, or the happy baby position: you relax and you have to let one go! That tiny squeak between the cheeks seems to echo around the studio, but fear not; no-one will know it's you, unless you're standing near a naked flame!

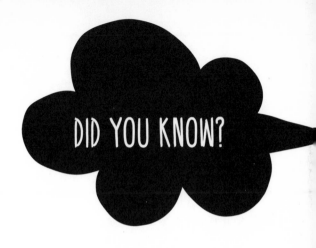

DID YOU KNOW?

Studies have suggested that
herring communicate by farting.
The noise, described by researchers
as being like a high-pitched raspberry,
is mostly used at night when the
fish are in a high-density shoal.

 # FART TENNIS

SMELLINESS RATING: 🪵🪵

LOUDNESS RATING: 🎺🎺🎺

MESSINESS RATING: 👙👙👙

OVERALL: ʕʔ ʕʔ ʕʔ

A game to be played with your
lover under the covers, but watch
for those power serves as you
might see more than chalk dust!

 # FLASH SMOG

SMELLINESS RATING:

LOUDNESS RATING:

MESSINESS RATING:

OVERALL:

A flash mob of farters, typically organised
via social media platforms such as Fartr,
Fartbook or Parpchat. If the crowd
is able to disperse before the smell
does, you know it's been a success.

HISTORICAL
FARTS

These are farts for the ages that have
been handed down through generations.
They connect us to our parping heritage
and take us back to a time when life
was simple and farts were stinky.

 # REAR ADMIRAL

SMELLINESS RATING:

LOUDNESS RATING:

MESSINESS RATING:

OVERALL:

Make sure you stand to attention when you blow this butt bugle — a most stately and upstanding fart. Even Admiral Nelson himself used this as a call to arms at the Battle of Trafalgar.

GUSTY GUSSET

SMELLINESS RATING:

LOUDNESS RATING:

MESSINESS RATING:

OVERALL:

Even English roses in costume dramas suffer from draughty derrieres. If you thought the swooning was caused by the arrival of Mr Ponsonby-Darcy-Havelock on a white charger, you are mistaken. It's the noxious farts that get trapped in the acres of taffeta that knock them out!

DID YOU KNOW?

Fart-lighting is the process whereby an individual holds an open flame near the fart exit zone and produces a 'Blue Angel' on expulsion. This name comes from gases produced in the colon which turn blue upon ignition. Beware though; this can be dangerous if it goes wrong, as evidenced by many a YouTube video.

# THE TOMB OF TOOT-ANKHAMUN

SMELLINESS RATING:

LOUDNESS RATING:

MESSINESS RATING:

OVERALL:

Release your Sphinx-ter and let out a fart that the pharaohs themselves would have been proud of.

FART-GATE

SMELLINESS RATING:

LOUDNESS RATING:

MESSINESS RATING:

OVERALL:

The sort of fart that could bring down a government. A fart heard around the world. A fart that could only be denied by the phrase, 'I did not have culinary relations with that burrito!'

 BLAZING SADDLES

SMELLINESS RATING: 🌭🌭🌭

LOUDNESS RATING: 🎺🎺

MESSINESS RATING: 👙👙👙

OVERALL: 💨 💨 💨

A hot, fiery fart usually experienced
after a hard day of rounding up cattle
and eating refried beans. You may
need to give your chaps and jeans a
bit of an airing out after this one.

FARTING ETIQUETTE

A truly magnificent situation to let one go is whilst skydiving. If you're a capable enough parachutist that you're able to do a solo jump, then you're free to let one fly and the fart trail will quickly disappear behind you as you hurtle to the earth. If you have an instructor strapped to your back, hope that they like you enough to still pull the chute after you've farted on their crotch...

THE ABRABUM LINCOLN

SMELLINESS RATING:

LOUDNESS RATING:

MESSINESS RATING:

OVERALL:

Four score and seven cans of beans ago, you brought forth in your digestive system a new odour, conceived in gluttony, and dedicated to the proposition that all farts are created equally smelly. Pull your stovepipe hat down tight and pray for emancipation.

MINI FARTS

These farts are testament to the
fact that good things do come in small
packages, because it's not the size of
the fart, it's what you do with it.

 # FUN-SIZE FLATULENCE

SMELLINESS RATING:

LOUDNESS RATING:

MESSINESS RATING:

OVERALL:

Perfect to pinch off when you don't have time for the lush, self-indulgent fart you're longing for. The fart of choice for high-powered businesspeople, busy waitstaff and anybody who can't catch a minute to cut the cheese.

POCKET PARP

SMELLINESS RATING:

LOUDNESS RATING:

MESSINESS RATING:

OVERALL:

It's the little things in life that mean the most — the first flower of spring, a smile from a baby... a teensy little Pocket Parp as you rouse from your slumber — it's almost like your sphincter is saying a cheery good morning.

 # SNEAKY SQUEAK

SMELLINESS RATING: 🪵🪵

LOUDNESS RATING: 🎺

MESSINESS RATING: ▽

OVERALL: ⑴⑴|

'Was that a mouse?'
'Why, yes.'
The Sneaky Squeak is a versatile trump,
and one that can be disguised with
minimum fuss at most social occasions,
apart from snooker tournaments where
you just have to hold your hand up.

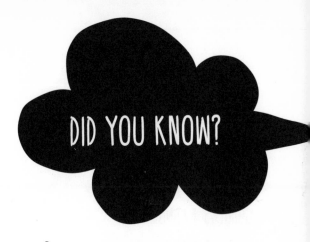

DID YOU KNOW?

On average, a person farts around
15 times a day, and most of these will
happen while sleeping. The total volume
of gas produced is 500 to 1,500 millilitres.

Farts have been measured to
travel at speeds of up to 10 feet
per second, or 7 miles per hour.

 # SQUEAKY FLOORBOARD

SMELLINESS RATING: 🪵🪵🪵

LOUDNESS RATING: 🎺

MESSINESS RATING: 👙

OVERALL: ᔑⅼ ᔑⅼ

A favourite among estate agents — and
if it's particularly pungent you can say
the drains might need looking at.

THE SOUND AND THE FURY

Get out those ear defenders and tell your granny to turn down her hearing aid: these are the farts that really push the decibels. Fart loud and fart proud!

THAR SHE BLOWS!

SMELLINESS RATING:

LOUDNESS RATING:

MESSINESS RATING:

OVERALL:

The grand-daddy of farts, and one that's usually performed by granddads and grandmas. They're sound asleep on the sofa after a big lunch, and before too long they start to snore from both ends.

 # TROUSER COUGH

SMELLINESS RATING:

LOUDNESS RATING:

MESSINESS RATING:

OVERALL:

Like a little yappy dog, but with no
dog in sight, this one is persistent.
Disguise it by looking around you
and calling out, 'Barnaby, come here
you naughty dog!' It might work.

SPHINCTER SONG

SMELLINESS RATING: 🎋🎋

LOUDNESS RATING: 🎺🎺🎺

MESSINESS RATING: 🩲

OVERALL: ⫤ ⫤

This is a love song from your bottom. For true masters, a key change for the last chorus will really tug heartstrings.

RECTAL SHOUT

SMELLINESS RATING:

LOUDNESS RATING:

MESSINESS RATING:

OVERALL:

This is a 12 on the Rectum Scale. Make for cover under the nearest door frame or table in the event of aftershocks.

DID YOU KNOW?

Maggots have long been used for cleaning wounds due to them eating only dead, not living, tissue, but now the medical application of the flatulence of maggots is being investigated. Their farts have been shown to have antibiotic properties.

MESSY FARTS

These are the farts your mother warned you about. None are to be attempted whilst sitting on a white sofa, or, for that matter, any furniture you don't want to throw out.

BROWN FAIRY DUST

SMELLINESS RATING:

LOUDNESS RATING:

MESSINESS RATING:

OVERALL:

Don't be fooled by the cute name, this one's a shitstorm! We're talking lockdown! Confine yourself to the smallest room, put on your rubber gloves and be prepared to make a bit of a mess. As farts go, this barely makes the fun-o-meter as, unless you're round your parents' house, you're going to have to clean it up yourself.

 # GLITTER BOMB

SMELLINESS RATING:

LOUDNESS RATING:

MESSINESS RATING:

OVERALL:

This is what happens when you get a bit too cocky and misjudge the force needed to expel your gas — you get poo glitter. It behaves in the same way as normal glitter except there's nothing sparkly about it.

 # RISKY BISCUIT

SMELLINESS RATING:

LOUDNESS RATING:

MESSINESS RATING:

OVERALL:

This fart is not to be trusted. It's even
odds whether a solid or gas should
be expected, and you won't know until
it's much, much too late. This one is
for desperados and daredevils only.

POWER SHOWER FART

SMELLINESS RATING: ▨▨▨▨

LOUDNESS RATING: 📯📯📯📯

MESSINESS RATING: 👙👙👙

OVERALL: ⸜| ⸜| ⸜| ⸜

We've all been there — you're in the shower, you're relaxed and daydreaming about the magical places the day might take you. Then, suddenly, a thunderous noise echoes around the cubicle. From whence? Your behind, of course. Be sure to check the surface behind you doesn't need a bit of a rinse off afterwards.

FARTING ETIQUETTE

For the horrors of a particularly loud fart, you have to get creative. Attempt to shuffle your shoe on the floor in the hopes that it too will squeak. If you know that it's approaching and there's nothing you can do to stop it, try to mask the sound with a hefty coughing fit.

# BEING CARTED OFF

SMELLINESS RATING:

LOUDNESS RATING:

MESSINESS RATING:

OVERALL:

An unexpected fart brought about by a hearty cough. This cough-fart hybrid (or 'cart') is very much a double-edged sword, as although the audio camouflage can come in handy, the completely involuntary nature of this fart can lead to it being a bit... messy.

THE SWAMP THING

SMELLINESS RATING:

LOUDNESS RATING:

MESSINESS RATING:

OVERALL:

A perfect tropical storm in your underpants. The right combination of humid weather, rich, spicy food and a sensitive stomach leading to unspeakable regret in opting for the white cotton trousers today.

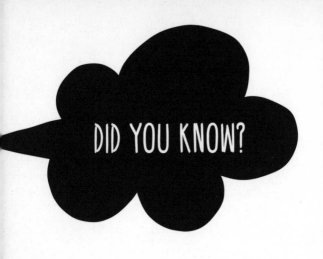

DID YOU KNOW?

Termite farts contribute between
2 and 22 trillion grams of methane
to the atmosphere every year.

ADVANCED
FARTING

This mixed bum-bag of farts is
full of expulsions only to be tried
by true experts in flatulence.

BROWN THUNDER

SMELLINESS RATING:

LOUDNESS RATING:

MESSINESS RATING:

OVERALL:

'Whoa there! You're going to frighten the horses!' is a cry you can expect to hear when you let off one of these decibel-laden underpant-scorchers. The element of danger, and the risk of a brown stain, means this is one for people who like to live on the edge. Volume can be easily adjusted by varying the sitting surface — metal and wood being particularly excellent amplifiers.

THE FOG

SMELLINESS RATING:

LOUDNESS RATING:

MESSINESS RATING:

OVERALL:

If you live within sight of a busy shipping lane, you'll need to hold this one in until you can dispose of it sensibly.

DID YOU KNOW?

The term 'raspberry', meaning to make
a sound like a fart with the mouth,
is an instance of rhyming slang, as
'fart' rhymes with 'raspberry tart'.

 # FREE JACUZZI

SMELLINESS RATING:

LOUDNESS RATING:

MESSINESS RATING:

OVERALL:

There's no need to go to the expense
of purchasing a top-of-the-range
bathroom suite when you can make
your own bottom bubbles — now's
not the time to follow through unless
you want to swim with poo fish.

SNAP, CACKLE AND... PLOP

SMELLINESS RATING:

LOUDNESS RATING:

MESSINESS RATING:

OVERALL:

This is the malodorous result of holding it in for too long as you shuffle uncomfortably on a chair, usually in one of those potentially life-changing moments, like when you're being interviewed for your dream job or making your debut appearance on *Question Time*. It's coming and you just can't stop it. It's like an earthquake in your pants – all you can do is laugh it off and then, just when you think you've got away with it, you suddenly feel taller and the chair is a bit damp.

SCOTCH MIST

SMELLINESS RATING: \\\\

LOUDNESS RATING:

MESSINESS RATING:

OVERALL:

No, that's not the distant sound of bagpipes echoing across the Highlands — it's a fart with the power to blur your vision and make you see fairies.

THE LEGENDS
OF FARTING

Some farts never die, but live on in
infamy. Farts of the originals, the icons
and the greats. These are those farts.

 # THE MARILYN

SMELLINESS RATING:

LOUDNESS RATING:

MESSINESS RATING:

OVERALL:

A sophisticated fart from a bygone era. Completely silent, yet with the force to send a long dress fluttering up around your ears. You didn't think that was wind from an air vent, did you?

THE JAGGER

SMELLINESS RATING:

LOUDNESS RATING:

MESSINESS RATING:

OVERALL:

Wearing skin-tight pants and strutting in six-inch heels is not going to stop one of these from rocking out of your anal passage — it's a gas, gas, gaaaaaaaassss!

 # THE ELVIS

SMELLINESS RATING:

LOUDNESS RATING:

MESSINESS RATING:

OVERALL:

A fart guaranteed to get scores of
teenage girls screaming and passing out.
Get your hips shaking and lip snarling and
let out a fart that'll leave you all shook
up. If you're met with any disapproving
glances, just blame it on the hound dog.

ANIMAL FARTS

If a bear farts in the forest, does he laugh? No. And that's what separates us from the animals. These farts all help to bridge the gap between man and beast.

CHIPMUNK

SMELLINESS RATING:

LOUDNESS RATING:

MESSINESS RATING:

OVERALL:

• •

This one has quite a guttural sound,
the way it stops and starts and you're
never sure if you've finished. It's like
your behind is chewing a toffee.

• •

THE WHALE SONG

SMELLINESS RATING:

LOUDNESS RATING:

MESSINESS RATING:

OVERALL:

A fart much like its namesake — majestic, mysterious and unhurried. A long, deep, sonorous fart that will carry for miles around. Be careful letting this one go in the bath as you may end up in an awkward conversation with a giant marine mammal you've never met.

 # BUFFALO

SMELLINESS RATING:

LOUDNESS RATING:

MESSINESS RATING:

OVERALL:

A big, beefy, woolly fart — the perfect
trump employed by many an after-
dinner speaker to sound the end of a
rousing speech, worthy of a standing
ovation in anybody's language.

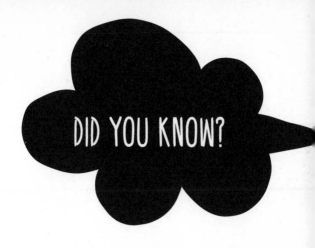

DID YOU KNOW?

The amount we fart can be increased by drinking fizzy drinks and chewing gum. This is because these two activities increase the amount of gas in our digestive system as we ingest the carbon dioxide in the drinks and swallow air whilst chewing the gum.

THE PARROT

SMELLINESS RATING:

LOUDNESS RATING:

MESSINESS RATING:

OVERALL:

A fart only to be attempted by true masters of the flatus. With this expulsion, the farter tries to imitate other sounds, like the unholy combination of Mr Pétomane (well-known French turn-of-the-century flatulist, or fart entertainer) and that guy from *Police Academy* who did the sound effects.

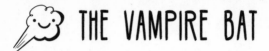 # THE VAMPIRE BAT

SMELLINESS RATING:

LOUDNESS RATING:

MESSINESS RATING:

OVERALL:

Generally nocturnal, this fart elicits a strong response from anyone who gets a whiff. Its stink is such that the blood will drain completely from their faces, leaving them pale and sickly. Legend has it that if you're 'bitten' by the Vampire Bat, you've only hours left before you turn, and fart one yourself...

THE RATTLE
SNAKE

SMELLINESS RATING:

LOUDNESS RATING:

MESSINESS RATING:

OVERALL: ६f| ६f| ६f| ६

A venomous fart, capable of causing
untold damage to anyone subjected
to it, emanating a hiss as it is slowly
released. By the time it's been smelt,
it's much too late; paralysis has
set in and death is inevitable.

THE NIGHT OWL

SMELLINESS RATING:

LOUDNESS RATING:

MESSINESS RATING:

OVERALL:

This one is a night-time toot that'll chill you to the bone. Pungent enough to make you turn your head all the way around and leave you wide-eyed and wide awake, wondering whether that noise was a spooky visitor outside your window or a stinky visitor inside your pants.

 # HYENA

SMELLINESS RATING:

LOUDNESS RATING:

MESSINESS RATING:

OVERALL:

This fart sounds like your anus is laughing at you, as if mocking you for trying to hold it in. It's a wild one, that's for sure.

THE FINAL FART

THE LONG
FART GOODNIGHT

SMELLINESS RATING: ▨ ▨ ▨

LOUDNESS RATING: 📯 📯 📯 📯

MESSINESS RATING: 👙

OVERALL: ᶘ ᶘᶘ ᶘᶘ ᶘ

For when a kiss isn't nearly enough...
Sure to leave a lasting impression!

THE LITTLE
BOOK OF
SHIT